Dolls

By
Ruth and Ed Radlauer

AN ELK GROVE BOOK

℗ CHILDRENS PRESS, CHICAGO

33865

Created by Radlauer Productions, Inc. for Childrens Press

For help with photographs and information,
the authors thank the following people:
   Clyde Hall of Grand Teton National Park,
   Barbara Gamble, Ann Galles, Jeanette Miller,
   and Doris Jacques of Casper, Wyoming,
   Bettina Shaw of Temecula, California,
   Una Blue of Hemet, California,
   and Pam Rutledge of Indio, California.

Library of Congress Cataloging in Publication Data

Radlauer, Ruth Shaw.
  Dolls.

  (Ready, get set, go)
  "An Elk Grove book."
  SUMMARY: Briefly discusses different types of dolls
  including those made of rags, apples, and child china.
    1. Dolls—Juvenile literature. I. Radlauer,
Edward, joint author. II. Title.
TS2301.T7R33   745.592'21   80-12247
ISBN 0-516-07777-5

   2 3 4 5 6 7 8 9 10 11 12 13 14 15 R 86 85 84 83 82 81 80

Ready, Get Set, Go Books

Ready

Motorcycle Mania
Flying Mania
Skateboard Mania
Shark Mania

Monkey Mania
Dinosaur Mania
Monster Mania
Roller Skate Mania

Get Set

Fast, Faster, Fastest
Wild Wheels
Racing Numbers
Boats

CB Radio
Model Trains
Trucks
Minibike Racing

Go

Soap Box Racing
Ready, Get Set, Whoa!
Model Airplanes
Model Cars

Soccer
Bicycle Motocross
Miniatures
Dolls

Just look! It's Raggedy Ann with
Raggedy Andy. Are they sister and
brother? We don't know for sure. We
are sure they're dolls, and dolls have
been around a long time.

A long time ago, cloth dolls were made of rags. People called them rag dolls. That's how Ann and Andy got their names, Raggedy Ann and Raggedy Andy.

Dolls that have been around a
long time are old, old enough to be
antiques. People like antiques so
much that they make copies of antiques.

How old is an antique doll? To
be antique, a doll must be 100 years
old or more. This Indian doll was
made some time between 1875 and 1900.
Is it an antique?

Indians made dolls from things
they found around them. Sticks,
cornhusks, leather, bits of cloth,
and beads made good Indian dolls.

Looking for an old doll? You
may find one in an antique store.
But you'll pay a lot of money. Where
else could you find an old doll?

Dolls often hide in old trunks.
Are they waiting for antique hunters
to find them? Maybe you'll find a
treasure in someone's old trunk.

This treasure was made in Germany
in about 1900. Her head is made of
china, the same thing some dishes are
made of. It's bisque china without
a shiny glaze.

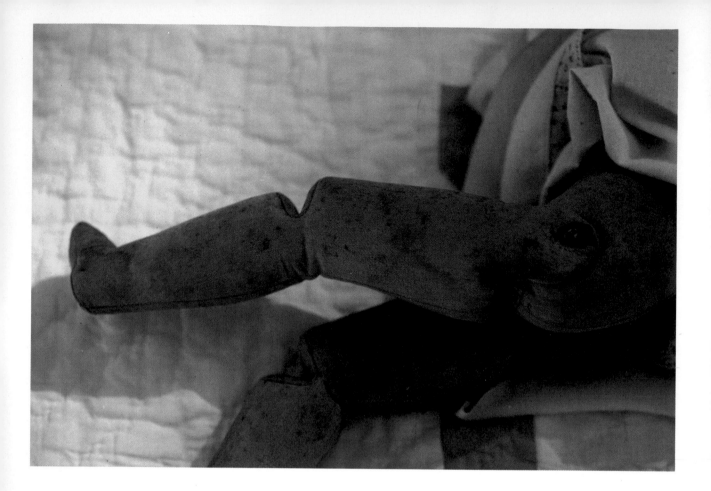

The German dollmaker gave the
china head a cloth body stuffed with
sawdust. The legs were made to bend
at the hip and knee.

Some dolls look like famous people.
The Jenny Lind doll looked like a famous
singer. The doll's head, hands, and
feet were made of a glazed china
called porcelain.

In the 1930s, everyone loved a
child movie star, Shirley Temple.
Many people wanted dolls that looked
like Shirley Temple.

The first Shirley Temple dolls
had blue eyes. But Ms. Temple's eyes
are brown. Later, this doll had brown
eyes, just like the real person's eyes.

Storybook dolls have always been
popular. The Marmee doll looks like
someone in the book, *Little Women.*
Marmee was the mother of four girls in
that story by Louisa May Alcott.

Scarlet O'Hara was a young southern
girl in the book, *Gone With the Wind.*
Scarlet O'Hara dolls with lovely green
eyes were made in the early 1940s.

What have we here? Prehistoric cave children's dolls? If they were, they'd be super antique. But these are plastic troll dolls popular in the 1960s.

Dolls can be made of plastic, china, rags—even—

—nuts! Take a pecan nut and
draw a face on it. Put hair and a
kerchief on top. The clothes go on
a wire body glued to the nut.

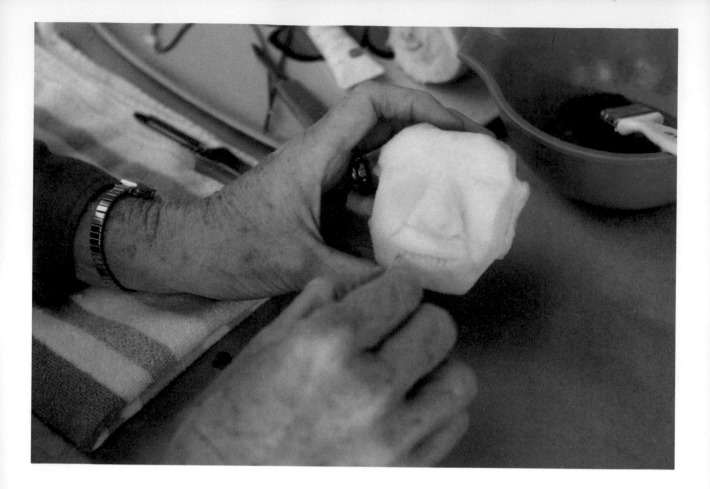

   Applehead dolls take a little more
work. First you peel an apple and
smooth it. Then you carve a face and
ears. It's OK to eat the parts you cut
away. Just don't eat the whole apple!

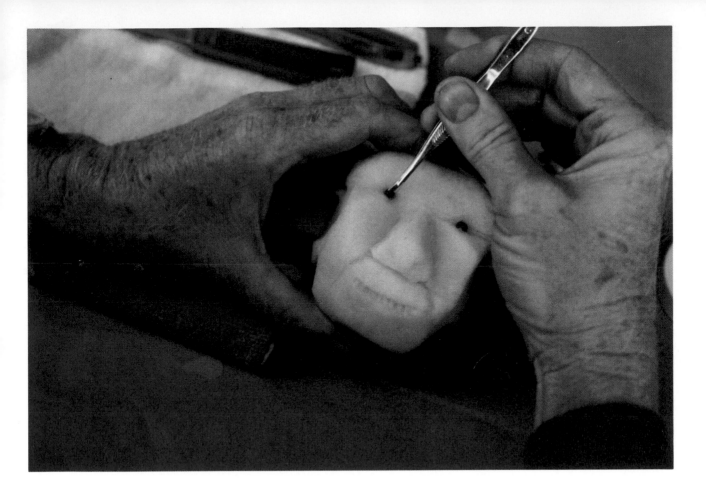

As you work, paint the apple with
lemon juice so it won't spoil. Grains
of rice make good teeth. Put cloves
or peppercorns in place for the eyes.

When you've carved the applehead, sprinkle lots of salt on it so it won't rot. Put a wire through the core and hang the apple in a dry place for about two weeks.

While you wait for the head to dry,
you can make a wire body. Wrap it with
cotton cloth strips cut from an old
T-shirt.

When the apple is dry, decide who
it's going to be. A man? A woman?
A football player? A fisherman? Then
you'll know how to dress the body.

Some collectors want dolls from other countries. A friend who travels to the Bahama islands or Canada may bring home a doll. Or a Greek store might have a doll from Greece.

An old Chinese doll with a china
head might be hiding in a trunk in
someone's attic. Since it's Chinese,
it has the costume of old China.

In Africa, where Zaire is, some
dolls are carved out of wood. The
Zaire costume is made of woven grass.

From Mexico comes a Mexican mother
doll. She carries a baby on her back.
Do you know a song she might sing to
her baby?

And then there's good old Uncle
Sam from the U.S.A. You know what songs
to sing for him!

When Grandmother was young, she
sang and sewed for Patsy Ann. Patsy
had a snowsuit for winter and beach
pajamas for summer.

And who dressed this teen-age doll?
Dolls like Barbie and her friends looked
like teen-age girls. Some even had
boyfriends.

Yes, people collect dolls, make
dolls, and sew clothes for them.
Does everyone like dolls? Do dolls
like to play with dolls?